INCREDIBLE JOURNEYS

New Zealand wildlife on the move

NED BARRAUD

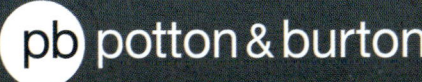
potton & burton

Have you ever wondered about the animals of Aotearoa that spend much of their lives travelling? There are many creatures that move from one place to another to find food, select a mate, breed and raise their young.

Because they are always on the go and often hidden, we don't usually see them. Where do they go? And why do they keep moving? This book will introduce you to some incredible animals that can travel thousands of kilometres – and never get lost.

Please remember that the maps in this book are very general, and are only meant to illustrate the kind of journeys these animals undertake – they do not depict actual routes.

CONTENTS

Papua
New Guinea

Solomon
Islands

Australia

New Caledonia

PACIFIC
OCEAN

Aotearoa

TASMAN SEA

4

SHINING CUCKOO PĪPĪWHARAUROA
THE NEST ROBBER

In autumn, the shining cuckoo/pīpī-wharauroa flies off from Aotearoa to the tropics around Papua New Guinea and the Solomon Islands. Here, it spends the winter, as it is warmer and there is plenty of food.

In spring, the pīpīwharauroa returns here, a flight of over 3000 kilometres, which is quite exceptional for a small forest bird.

Once they are here, despite their bright colouring they are very hard to see, but you might be able to hear their distinctive repeating whistle from somewhere high in the treetops.

The cuckoo is a brood parasite, which means it lays its egg in another bird's nest. In New Zealand, the grey warblers are the foster parents. The warbler provides the nest, hatches the egg and raises the cuckoo as its own.

LEATHERBACK SEA TURTLE HONU
WORLD-RECORD HOLDER

There are so many reasons why the leatherback turtle is amazing. It is a very old reptile and has been around since the dinosaurs.

It is the largest of the seven species of sea turtle – up to 3 metres long, weighing over 900 kilograms. It swims the fastest – its big flippers propel it to speeds of 35 kilometres an hour. And it is the turtle that dives the deepest – down to more than a kilometre, staying underwater for four to seven hours before coming to the surface to breathe.

It is the only sea turtle not to have a hard shell: the leatherback's shell is flexible, and made of a rubbery, oily thick skin.

It travels further than any other sea turtles. Some have been tracked making journeys of over 19,000 kilometres from the tropics where they breed to their feeding grounds in colder waters. The map shows the various journeys that leatherback turtles make.

How do sea turtles know where they are going? It remains a mystery, but satellite tags placed on their backs show that they migrate to New Zealand to feed, mainly on jellyfish and salps (jelly-like creatures that look like fish eggs).

Some spend more than a year in Aotearoa's waters but, because they don't usually come close to land, they are rarely spotted.

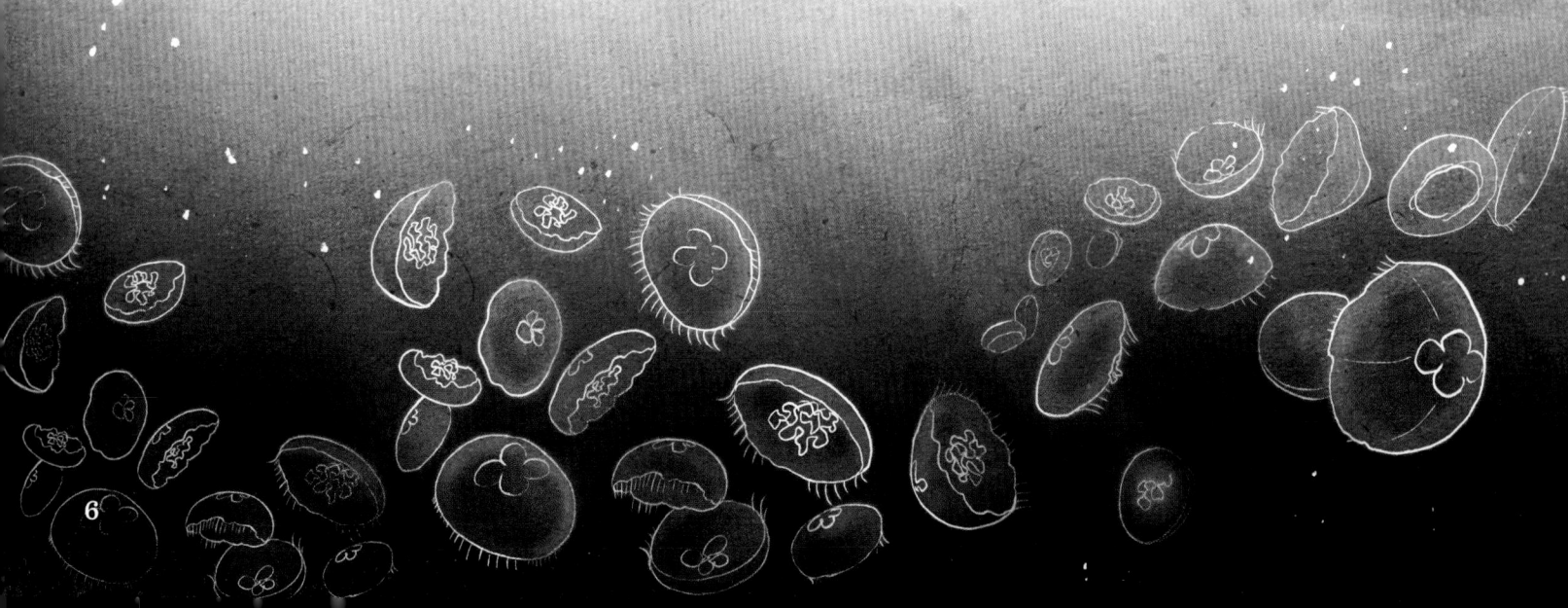

United States

Philippines

Indonesia

Costa Rica

PACIFIC
OCEAN

Australia

South
America

Aotearoa

BLACK PETREL TĀIKO
YOUNG, SOLO TRAVELLER

Black petrels/tāiko breed in inland burrows, with Aotearoa's largest colony of around 10,000 birds on Mt Hobson on Aotea/Great Barrier Island.

Their life journey begins when the young birds (fledglings) clumsily climb up trees to launch off. Some crash land and have to try again while others manage to soar away on their first ever flight, an epic 12,000 kilometres to fishing grounds near the Galápagos Islands in the Pacific Ocean.

These young birds remain at sea for four to six years before returning to Aotearoa to breed. Black petrels were once common in the North Island and northwest Nelson region. Now they are considered 'nationally vulnerable', which means they could face extinction if we don't look after them.

Their nest burrows are invaded by rats, cats or dug up by wild pigs. At sea, they are accidentally caught by commercial and recreational fishers.

Galápagos
Islands

Peru

**South
America**

EAST
PACIFIC
OCEAN

Aotea/Great Barrier
Island

Aotearoa

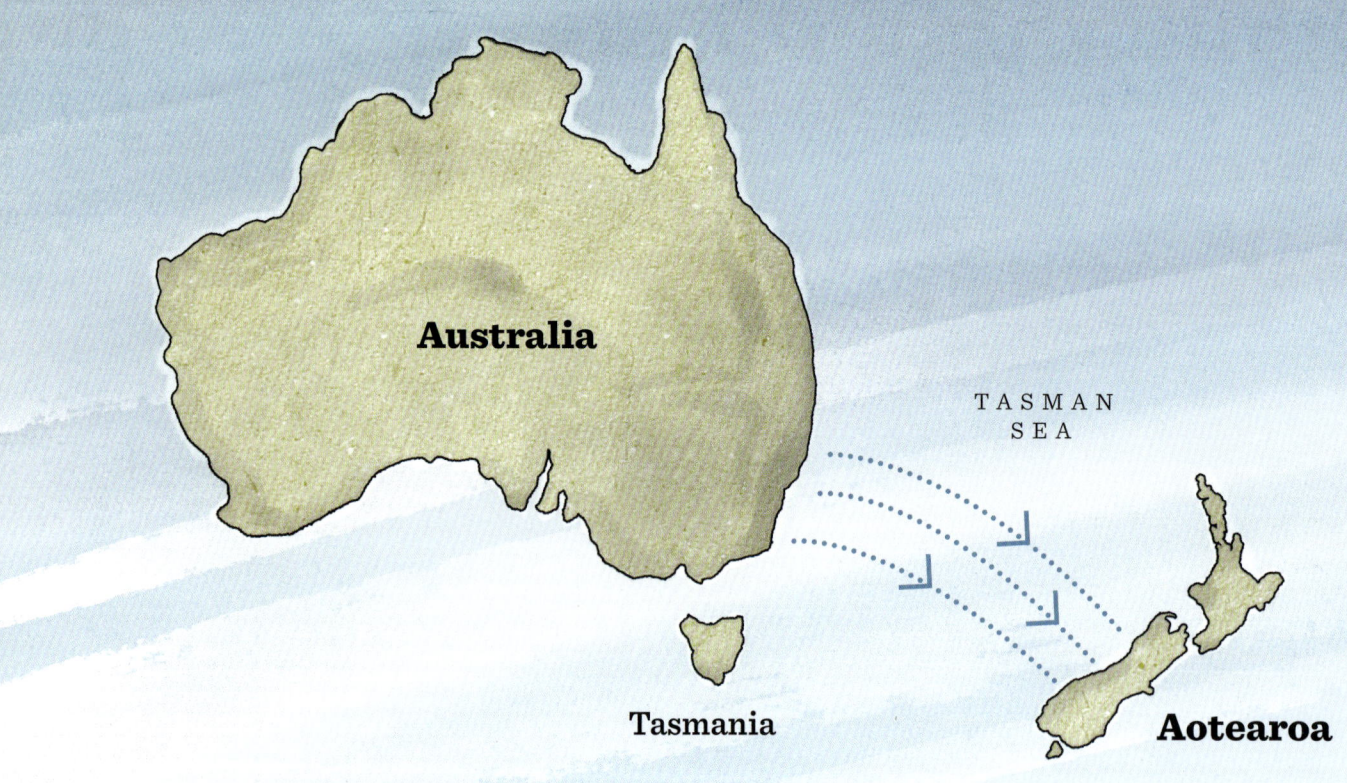

Australia

TASMAN
SEA

Tasmania

Aotearoa

BLUE MOON BUTTERFLY PŪREREHUA
WINGING IT

For millions of years, insects and birds have been swept across the Tasman Sea from Australia on strong westerly winds. Many don't survive the challenges faced with adapting to the new environment, but others find a home in Aotearoa.

Every year, the blue moon butterfly is blown here in late summer and autumn from Australia. That is over 4200 kilometres of travel! Although a rare species, they can be found throughout the country, particularly on the West Coast.

This beautiful butterfly has a wingspan of up to 100 millimetres. The male is black, with purplish-blue spots, while the female's wings have white marking and brownish-black wings.

Typically, they don't survive the harsh winter conditions and die off. But who knows, with a warming climate, they might find a more permanent home here.

CRAYFISH KŌURA
TIME FOR A LONG WALK

It seems as if crayfish hardly ever keep still. Once they hatch from under their mother's tail, they spend the next 18 months drifting out at sea until, somehow, they know how to come back to the coast.

And as adults, they're always on the move, but sometimes there is what is known as a mass migration – huge groups of kōura moving with the currents and crawling along the seafloor for hundreds of kilometres around the coastline of Aotearoa.

One tagged crayfish made a journey of 850 kilometres from Otago to Fiordland, but other migrations might be even longer than this.

How do they know where to go? Kōura have eyes that stick up on stalks and antennae to touch and explore what is around them. They have a strong sense of smell to help them locate their food. They can swim backwards using their tails but mostly they walk along the seafloor.

TASMAN
SEA

PACIFIC
OCEAN

Fiordland

Milford Sound

Dunedin

**Otago
Peninsula**

Invercargill

Stewart Island / Rakiura

When a longfin eel knows that it is time to breed, things start to change. It stops feeding, its eyes and fins get larger, its head becomes flatter and its belly becomes more silver in colour. Then it leaves the rivers and lakes of Aotearoa for a great journey, swimming for six months over 2000 kilometres to the tropical waters of the Pacific Ocean. Here, far below the surface, these adults die, but only after the females release vast amounts of eggs, to be fertilised by the males.

Once these millions of eel eggs hatch, they float to the surface, become larvae, and drift back to New Zealand on ocean currents. Here they turn into small, young 'glass eels' and move into river mouths and estuaries. Now as 'elvers', they are darker in colour, and are big, wriggly, long and slippery with a thick layer of slime on their skin. They can even climb vertical surfaces such as waterfalls and dams. They swim up waterways to find a suitable freshwater home where they can live for many years – some females can live to 100 years, grow up to 2 metres long and weigh over 20 kilograms.

hatching area

Vanuatu

Fiji

Tonga

New Caledonia

PACIFIC
OCEAN

eel larvae

adult eels

TASMAN
SEA

Aotearoa

BAR-TAILED GODWIT KUAKA
NON-STOP FLYER

The bar-tailed godwit is an extraordinary bird. From its breeding grounds in Alaska, it makes the longest non-stop flight of any bird on earth, flying for about eight days without any rest or inflight snacks along the way, 12,000 kilometres across the Pacific Ocean.

Hundreds of them arrive in September into Aotearoa, spending the summer feeding in harbours and estuaries all over the country.

When it is time to leave again for Alaska, generally in March, the godwits take off in groups of up to 25. They go a different route, stopping over for about five weeks on the Yellow Sea mudflats and estuaries off the coast of China and Korea. Once well fed and ready to fly again, they are off, arriving back in Alaska in good condition and ready for the Arctic summer breeding season.

Alaska

Korea Japan

NORTH
PACIFIC OCEAN

SOUTH
PACIFIC OCEAN

Australia

Aotearoa

HUMPBACK WHALE TOHORĀ
AN EPIC JOURNEY

Every year groups or 'pods' of humpback whales/tohorā pass by the coast of Aotearoa on their seasonal migration. They travel up to 10,000 kilometres, one of the longest migratory journeys of any mammal on earth.

Humpback whales spend the summer months in Antarctica feeding on krill and schools of small fish.

In autumn, they return to the warm waters of the South Pacific. Here, they spend the winter, breeding and giving birth to their calves.

All southern hemisphere humpback populations are slowly recovering after being hunted almost to extinction. Whaling for profit was finally made illegal worldwide in 1986, but whaling in New Zealand waters stopped in 1964.

Australia

SOUTH
PACIFIC
OCEAN

Aotearoa

SOUTHERN
OCEAN

Antarctica

19

TASMAN SEA

Aotearoa

SOUTH
PACIFIC
OCEAN

Taiaroa Head

Chatham
Islands

Auckland
Islands

Bounty Islands

Campbell
Island

Antipodes
Islands

SOUTHERN
OCEAN

NORTHERN ROYAL ALBATROSS TOROA
THE OCEAN WANDERER

One of the largest birds in the world is the northern royal albatross/toroa, with a wingspan of up to 3 metres. Their mainland breeding colony is at Taiaroa Head, near Dunedin, and from here they travel vast distances to feed throughout the Southern Ocean and in the waters off South America.

These incredible flyers can soar and glide as much as 190,000 kilometres in a year, riding the updrafts of air coming off the ocean waves, which means they hardly need to flap their wings.

The female lays a single large egg around December. Both parents take turns sitting on the egg, and when it hatches, they feed the chick until it is ready to fly off in October. The map shows a parent's possible flight-path when gathering food for its chick.

The northern royal albatross is one of the longest-living birds in the world. One female living on Taiaroa Head colony, nicknamed 'Grandma', reached the age of 62.

They are most commonly seen in our coastal waters over winter. If you're lucky you might spot a royal albatross as you cross Cook Strait on the ferry.

TAWAKI FIORDLAND CRESTED PENGUIN
HIDE AND SEEK

There are 18 species of penguin in the world, six of which breed in New Zealand.

One of the rarest is the tawaki/Fiordland crested penguin. It is a very timid bird and little is known about it. This is partly because it nests in thick rainforest, sea caves or under boulders – anywhere that is well hidden.

Recently, researchers used satellite tags to track 20 West Coast tawaki. They were astonished to find that they travel the greatest distance of any of the penguin species. Each December, after they finish rearing their chicks, the adult birds set off into the Southern Ocean to catch fish and to fatten up before the annual moult.

They cover distances of up to 7000 kilometres and spend 60–80 days away.

Australia

SOUTH
PACIFIC OCEAN

TASMAN
SEA

Aotearoa

SOUTHERN
OCEAN

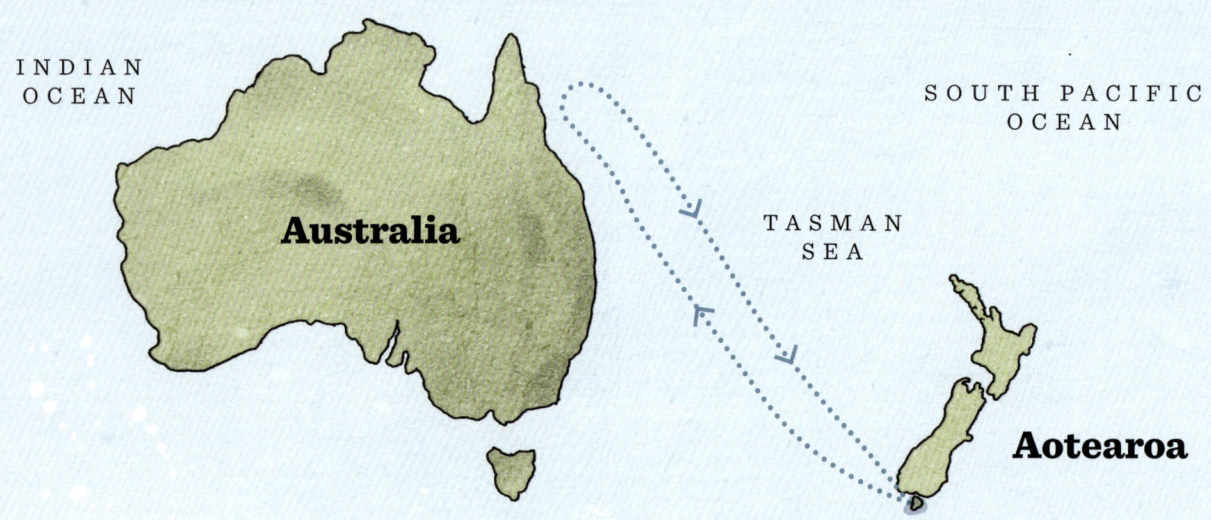

INDIAN
OCEAN

Australia

SOUTH PACIFIC
OCEAN

TASMAN
SEA

Aotearoa

Stewart Island / Rakiura

WHITE SHARK MANGŌ
APEX PREDATOR

White sharks/mangō are known as apex predators, which means they are at the top of the food chain. Their diet includes fur seals, stingrays, penguins, large fish and whale carcasses. But they are actually a vulnerable species because many sharks die in fishing nets every year, and their population is very slow to grow.

The white sharks that live around Stewart Island/Rakiura have been studied by scientists to understand where they go and when.

Satellite tagging has shown that the juveniles and adults migrate thousands of kilometres to warm tropical waters in March. They spend up to seven months far to the north of New Zealand off the coast of Australia and in the tropics before returning, often to the exact place where they were tagged. One tagged shark showed that they can cover 1000 kilometres of ocean in only one week.

25

SOOTY SHEARWATER TĪTĪ
SUMMER BREEZE

Scientists believe there are approximately 20 million sooty shearwaters in the world, but they are still threatened by over-fishing and a changing climate, both of which means there is less food for them to eat.

Around half of this huge population breeds in New Zealand, especially on colonies on Stewart Island /Rakiura, the Snares, Auckland Islands and other islands and a few headlands throughout the country, but mainly in the south.

The sooty shearwaters/tītī make the biggest migration of any animal ever recorded. Each year they fly 65,000 kilometres in a giant round-trip that gives them an endless summer. They make stops along the way to feed on small fish like anchovy and sardines.

Some go to locations off Japan, while others feed off the coast of Alaska or California before returning to New Zealand to breed.

Japan

United States

NORTH PACIFIC OCEAN

Australia

SOUTH PACIFIC OCEAN

Aotearoa

Snares Islands

Auckland Islands

I've often thought about where animals journey and why, and I've been very lucky to encounter many of these magnificent creatures shown in this book. My most memorable meeting was with a group of tawaki on Stewart Island/Rakiura. It was about 1998 and I was doing the nine-day coastal walk with my best mate Zack. On the southern tip of the track, we spotted some tawaki emerging from the sea and hopping over the rocks. I think these guys hadn't seen many humans before, they weren't in the least bit afraid and came right up close. I was surprised at how large they were. I'll never forget that as I crouched there, one of these big penguins sneezed right in my face. I could even smell its fishy breath!

NED BARRAUD

Other titles by the author:

'Explore and Discover' series
Animals of Aotearoa
New Zealand's Backyard Beasts
Moonman
Watch out for the Weka
Tohorā: the southern right whale
Rockpools: a Guide for Kiwi Kids
Where is it?
What happened to the moa
New Zealand's Backyard Birds

Published in 2021 by Potton & Burton
319a Hardy Street, PO Box 221
Nelson, New Zealand
www.pottonandburton.co.nz

© Ned Barraud

Layout/typography: Floor van Lierop

ISBN 978 1 98 855028 2 (softcover)
ISBN 978 1 98 855029 9 (hardcover)

Printed in China by Everbest Printing Co. Ltd